Wolves for Kids

By Tom Wolpert

NorthWord
PRESS, INC

Box 1360
Minocqua, WI 54548

Copyright© 1990

NorthWord Press, Inc.
Box 1360
Minocqua, WI 54548

For a free catalog describing NorthWord's line of nature and children's books and gifts, call 1-800-336-5666.

Design by Origins Design, Inc.

ISBN 1-55971-087-X (Hardcover)

ISBN 1-55971-123-X (Softcover)

Library of Congress Cataloging-in-Publication Data

Wolpert, Tom, 1947-
      Wolves for kids / by Tom Wolpert.
          p. cm.
      Summary: An introduction to the furry predator, focusing on where wolves live, why they howl, and how they communicate.
          ISBN 1-55971-123-X : $6.95
          1. Wolves--Juvenile literature. (1. Wolves.) I. Title.
QL737.C22W647   1991
599.74'442--dc20   91-17692
                                                       CIP
                                                        AC

PHOTO CREDITS:
Robert W. Baldwin, pp. 6, 30; Daniel J. Cox, pp. 3, 7, 12-13,
14, 22, 24-25, 44-45; Lynn Rogers, cover, pp. 4, 8, 9, 10, 16,
18-19, 20, 26, 28, 31, 32-33, 34-35, 36, 38, 40, 41, 42, 46.

The wolf is an animal we have heard about in fables and fairy tales. Because of those tales, we sometimes think the wolf is a ferocious animal that attacks and eats humans. But this is not true. In fact, the wolf is the *ancestor* of man's oldest animal friend - the dog.

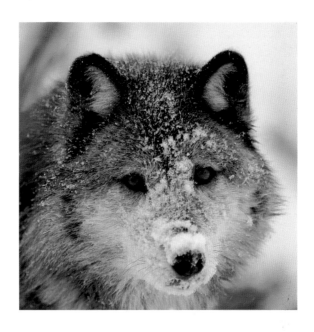

Almost all wolves in North America belong to a species called the gray wolf. A wolf looks like a large shaggy version of a German Shepherd, but a wolf has longer legs and larger feet. A wolf's head is larger and more rounded. Its eyes are set further apart. The cheeks of a wolf bulge with jaw muscles.

Male wolves are usually two and a half to three feet tall and weigh seventy-five to one hundred pounds. The largest wolf ever found weighed 175 pounds. Wolves this large are rare. Female wolves are smaller than males. They are usually one and a half to two and a half feet tall. A female wolf weighs sixty to eighty pounds. Wolves in Canada and Alaska are larger than wolves in the southern United States.

Wolves are found in many colors. Their color depends on their *environment*. Wolves are most often colored gray. However, some may be brown, golden brown, rusty red or almost any combination of these colors. Some are all black and others pure white. The arctic wolf is pure white.

The belly and throat of the wolf is usually light in color and almost white. The wolf's legs, ears and nose are often light brown. The face and back are usually marked with dark brown or black.

The timber wolf is often called the "gray wolf" because of its thick gray fur. The wolves of central Canada are usually gray. Wolves that live in the treeless plains of northern arctic regions and forests of Canada and Alaska may also be gray. Because of this, scientists have nicknamed all wolves that live in North America the gray wolf.

There are many wolves that live in the forests of Alaska, Canada, and northern Minnesota. A few wolves also live in upper Michigan and northern Wisconsin. These wolves are called "timber wolves" because they live among the trees. Most timber wolves are dark gray or black. Their home in the forest is shadowy and dark. The wolves' dark coats provide excellent *camouflage*.

Wolves that live in northern Alaska and Canada are called "tundra wolves." They live on the treeless plains or tundra. Tundra wolves are the most beautiful wolves in North America. They have beautiful thick fur to protect them from the cold. Some of these wolves are pure white so they can hide easily in the snow.

A few wolves still live in Arizona, Arkansas, Mississippi, Missouri, New Mexico and North Dakota. These wolves are smaller than those that live in the far north. They are gray in color.

The red wolf is a different species from the gray wolf. The red wolf lives in wilderness areas of Texas and Louisiana. The red wolf is nearly *extinct*.

Today in the United States, the gray wolf remains in large numbers only in Alaska and northern Minnesota. Between 5,000 and 15,000 wolves live in Alaska. About 1,200 wolves live in northern Minnesota.

In late winter where gray wolves live, the lakes are frozen and snow still covers the ground. Females wolves are able to become pregnant for only a few days during this time. During her first mating season, a young female will choose a mate that will be her partner for life. If one of the couple should die, the other one usually will never mate again.

The pregnant female begins digging a den three to four weeks before her pups arrive. She often searches several days to find the right spot. Her den must be on high ground so water does not seep into it. She may also choose a rock cave or even a hollow log for her den. However, the den must be near a river or a stream. This is important. Once the female starts to nurse her young, she will need to drink a lot of water.

Wolf dens are quite large. The front entrance is large enough for a man to crawl through. A tunnel leads from the entrance to the chamber where the pups are kept. The tunnel may be six to fourteen feet long. The chamber is large enough for the mother to stand in. Sometimes there are two chambers, one for the pups and one for the mother to rest in.

Sixty to sixty-two days after the parent wolves mate, the pups are born. Newborn wolves are called pups. While waiting for the pups to be born, the entire wolf family to which the parent wolves belong stays close to the den. This family, or pack, hunts for food close by the den instead of going on long hunts.

The day before the pups arrive, the female goes inside the den and stays until the pups are born. Her mate stands guard outside the entrance.

In the darkness of the den, the pups are born. Baby wolves are born deaf and with their eyes closed. Usually there are from four to seven pups in a litter.

Each pup weighs about one pound at birth. For the first ten or twelve days after their birth, they do nothing but nurse and sleep. The mother leaves the den only to drink. Her mate brings food to her.

The newborn pups are now members of the pack. Packs are family groups. Every wolf is born into a pack. The most basic pack will include a father, mother and a litter of pups. The leader of the pack is almost always a male. The leader will decide when the pack can go on a hunt. He will also decide when the pack can rest. All other wolves in the pack obey the leader.

When a pack makes a kill, the wolves wait and let the leader have the first choice of meat. Once he starts eating, the others join and begin to feed too.

When a pack is ready to rest after feeding, they follow the leader to the resting spot of his choice. When he is done resting and ready to move on, he walks up to the other members of the pack and wakes them.

There is also a female leader of the pack. She is in charge of all the other females in the pack. Sometimes she helps the male leader make the other wolves obey his commands. The male leader is usually the chief wolf in the whole pack. However, when the male and female leaders have pups, the female becomes the head wolf. She remains the head wolf

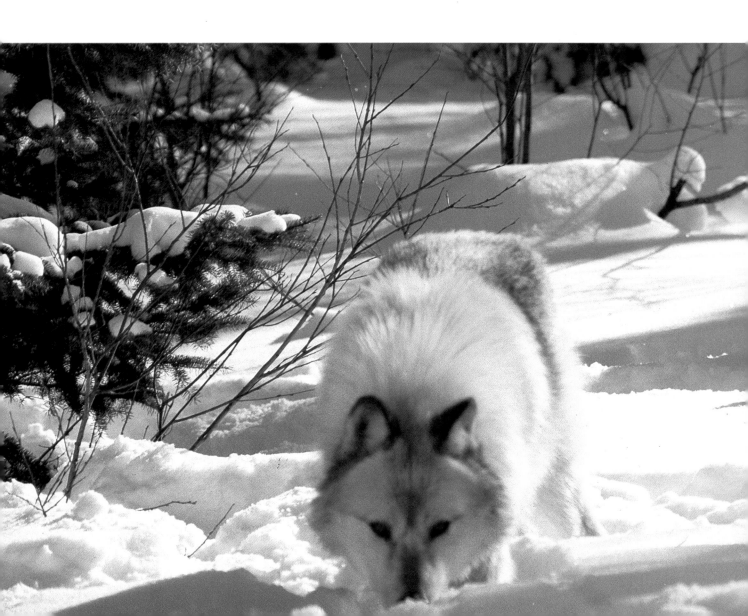

until her pups are old enough to travel and hunt with the pack. Then the father wolf becomes the head wolf once again.

Some wolf packs have as many as thirty-six members. In these large packs there are many adults. However, there is still only one male and female leader.

About two weeks after they are born, the pups are able to open their eyes. They learn to stand and then to walk. Their front teeth come in at this time. Now they begin chewing on each other's tails. By the time they are three weeks old, they can hear and see very well. Now it is time for them to go outside the den for the first time.

The other pack members become very excited when they see the pups for the first time. The pack members wag their tails and gather around the pups and lick them. This is the first time the father is able to get close to his pups.

All the wolves are very protective of pups in the pack. During the next several months, the pups spend a lot of time playing outside the den. Many pack members will take turns standing guard over the pups. If the mother must leave to get food, another adult will "baby-sit" the pups for her.

When the pups are about four weeks old, they begin to eat solid food. When an adult wolf returns from eating a meal, the pups swarm around it. The adult then ejects the food in its stomach in front of the hungry pups. The pups then eat this food that was brought to them in the stomach of the adult wolf.

Carrying the meat back in their stomachs has advantages for the adult wolves. If the wolf carried the meat back in its mouth, the food would get covered with dust, sand and dirt. Also the smell of the meat would leave a scent trail for other animals to follow to the den. A bear, wolverine, fisher or lynx could follow the trail and kill the young pups. So when the adult wolves bring the meat back in their stomachs, the meat arrives fresh, warm, undigested, and clean. Also, the location of the den remains a secret from other animals.

The pups begin to learn the ways of adult wolves when they are about three months of age. Then the mother no longer allows the pups to sleep in the den. The pups begin to sleep outside with the rest of the wolves. When the pups begin to sleep outside, the other wolves in the pack begin to go on longer hunts. Several of the younger adult wolves stay behind with the pups. After several days, the pack returns to the den area and the waiting pups.

Wolves are master hunters. Wolves eat very large animals or many small animals, depending on what type of *prey* is available. Wolves kill sick or injured caribou, moose or deer that would be a burden to the rest of their herd. The wolves will travel miles in search of food for themselves and their

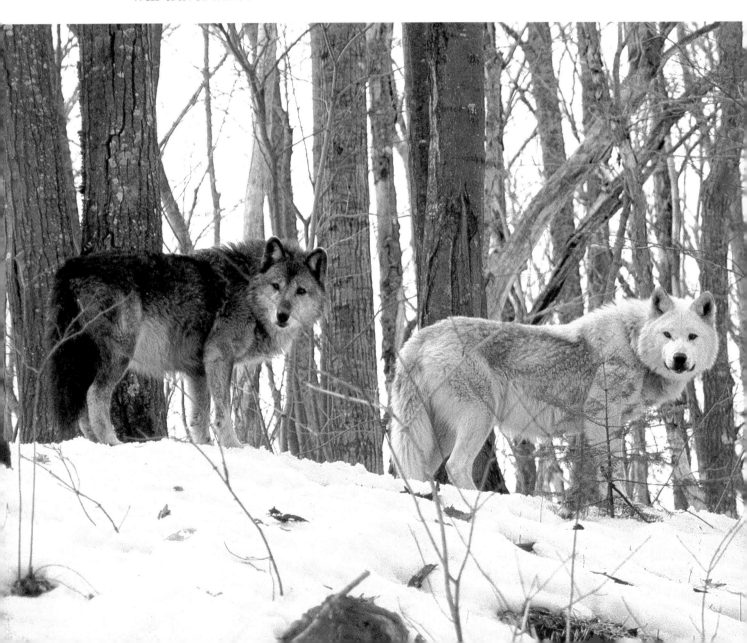

young pups. The timber wolf often travels along the tops of ridges when hunting. From the tops of these ridges the wolves can look down for prey. When the prey is spotted, the wolves rush down to capture it.

The wolf is a powerful runner. It can run for long distances. However, it cannot run at very high speeds. A wolf can outrun a man, but has trouble overtaking hoofed animals. Wolves solve this problem by hunting in packs. Hunting in packs allows the wolves to circle their prey. The prey is then caught in the middle and cannot run from the wolves.

A wolf can survive for two weeks without eating. During this time it will hunt and chase many animals. Finally it will find one it can kill.

Wolves journey far and wide while hunting. The pack usually travels in single file. They travel about 5 miles an hour. They travel on frozen waterways, windswept ridges, and old roads and trails in search of food.

The pack may have to travel many miles in a day to find a herd of animals to prey upon. Wolves always travel at a steady trot and rarely walk. Wolves can travel forty miles without rest.

Wolves track down prey animals by using their keen sense of smell. As the pack gets closer to the herd of prey animals, the smell of the prey gets stronger. Wolves do not rush in at the herd. They stay back and study it. The pack looks for an animal that is old, sick or very young. These animals cannot run as fast. The pack knows these animals are easier to catch.

Wolves actually help keep herds of deer and other animals healthy. Killing the old or sick members of a herd leaves more food for the other herd members. With more food, the healthy animals are able to have strong, healthy young.

Once wolves make a kill, they can eat a large amount. The expression - "to eat like a wolf" - comes from their eating habits. A healthy adult wolf can eat twenty pounds of meat at one feeding.

When the pack has finished eating the meat, they wander off to a sunny place to rest. After sleeping for several hours, they return to their kill. After eating any meat that is left, they spend hours chewing on the bones. This keeps their teeth clean and strong. It also supplies them with necessary minerals.

Wolves are very good communicators. They use sounds and gestures to "show talk" to other members in their pack. Wolves can make a variety of sounds. Each sound has its own meaning. If a wolf is restless or excited, it whimpers. Wolves also whimper when they bring food to the pups.

A snarl means that a wolf is threatening another wolf. It is a warning. It is a way of telling other wolves that they are making the snarling wolf unhappy.

A short "wuff" is a warning sound. When a member of the pack senses danger, it makes a "wuff" sound. If the danger becomes stronger, the "wuff" turns into a bark. When pack members hear a bark, they know it is time to flee.

The wolf is probably best known for its howling. A wolf howling alone produces a low, mournful cry. When several wolves howl together, their voices blend together. Some wolves also yip and some yowl. Others moan, whine, bark or wail.

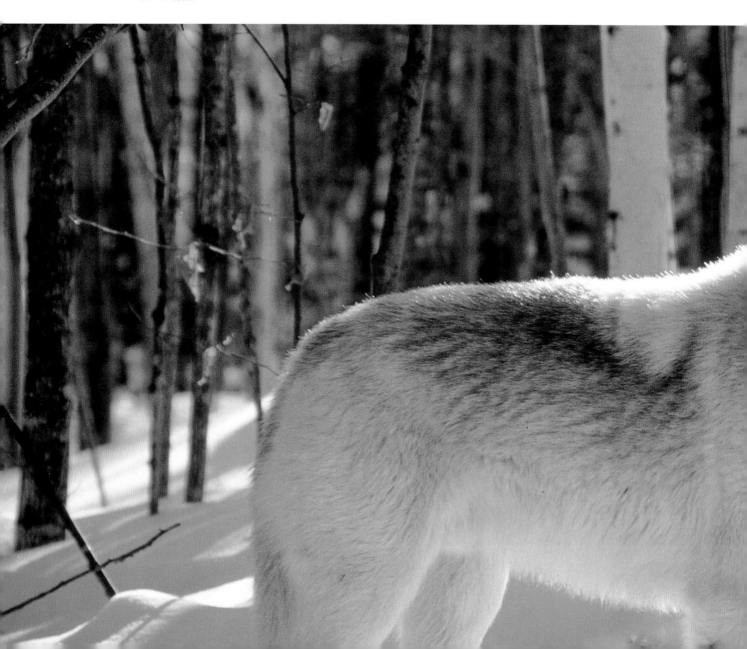

Scientists do not know why wolves howl. Some people say wolves howl because they are lonely. Others say wolves howl to find other wolves. However, most scientists agree that wolf packs howl to tell other wolf packs to stay away from their territory. This howling also helps to bond the pack together.

Only in recent years have we begun to understand the wolf. Wolves are interesting and beautiful animals. Ordinarily, wolves are afraid of people and will flee from humans. Not one case of healthy wolves attacking people has been recorded in North America.

As we have begun to learn more about our environment, we have learned that the wolf plays an important role in nature. Where the wolf lives, it helps keep prey animals from becoming so *abundant* that they starve or die of disease. When the prey animals are not abundant, the wolves do not have pups. That way, the number of wolves stays small, and the wolves do not have to share what little meat they can catch with pups.

Wolves must kill other animals in order to live. But like eagles and foxes and bears and other *predators* that also eat animals, the wolf and its prey have survived and lived together in the same places for many thousands of years.

Index

Here's a list of the *italicized* words in the text, followed by the page number where each word first appears.

Abundant: (Page 47) Being in plentiful supply.

Ancestor: (Page 5) A family relative from long ago.

Camouflage: (Page 11) A way to hide by blending in with the surrounding area.

Environment: (Page 9) The surroundings of an animal, including the landscape, weather and food conditions.

Extinct: (Page 13) No longer in existence as a species.

Predators: (Page 47) Animals that live by eating other animals.

Prey: (Page 34) A creature hunted or caught for food.

Parent/Child Interaction Questions

Parents: *These are questions you may ask your children in order to get them to think about wolves as viable occupants of a niche in the food chain. Encourage them to explain their feelings about wolves, and to ask their own questions. Clarify any misunderstandings they may have about the predators, and explain the need to have both predators and prey in the world. In this way, you can help foster future generations of environmentally aware and appreciative adults. If you would like more in-depth information about wolves, there are other NorthWord titles that may interest you:* White Wolf *by Jim Brandenburg,* Guide To Northwoods Wildlife *by Janine Benyus.*

1. Why do you think wolves need coats that provide good camouflage?

2. How are wolf pups and human babies alike?

3. Why do you think the mother wolf no longer allows the pups to sleep in the den after they are three months old?

4. Why do you think people have made up scary stories about wolves? Do you think wolves are bad? Why or why not?

5. Would you like to belong to a wolf pack? Why or why not?